MONEY
MANAGEMENT

DISCOVER HOW TO GET OUT OF DEBT,
CREATE A BUDGET, SAVE MONEY, MAKE MONEY ALL
WHILE BUILDING REAL WEALTH

BONUS INCLUDED:
20 Principles of Financial Abundance!

JACK GRAY

GET YOUR

FREE GIFT!

WAIT! – DO YOU LIKE FREE BOOKS?

My **FREE Gift** to You!! As a way to say **Thank You** for downloading my book, I'd like to offer you more **FREE BOOKS!** Each time we release a NEW book, we offer it first to a small number of people as a test–drive. Because of your commitment here in downloading my book, I'd love for you to be a part of this group. You can join easily here → http://yourcashmanagement.com/

Table of Contents

Chapter 1

How Hitting Rock Bottom Saved My Life

My Background Story

Welcome

It is incredibly easy to lose control of your finances. Make a few bad choices, and if you don't have the knowledge about how to repair the damage, the situation can quickly spiral out of control. That's exactly what happened to me.

So, who am I? My name is Jack Gray, and I'm not afraid to admit that I've made my share of mistakes. My hope is that by writing this book, I can help you avoid some of the pitfalls that I walked straight into. There is a huge amount of misinformation out there when it comes to managing your money. There are a lot of gurus who purport to have a 'new' method for making you rich, getting you out of debt, giving you financial 'freedom' or whatever other catch phrase seems to be popular on a given week.

I'm not here to preach a method to you. I'm here to share tips that worked for me as I dug myself out from the massive hole that I found myself in. I've tried all the tips, all the schemes and all the methods, some which worked, some which didn't. It's possible that not everything in this book will work for you, and that's FINE. However, I am 100% sure that if you work your way through this book, you will find dozens of tips and ideas that will work for you. Keep those, hone in on them, stick with them, and you can quickly gain control of your financial well being.

Meet Jack

My story.

I was living in the dream. I had an MBA in my pocket and a fairly high-paying job right out of school. As far as I was concerned, life was perfect. So what did I do?

I went out and got all the things that I thought I needed to make my life even more perfect. I bought a house, a car, great clothes, great furniture, I went out to dinner all the time, took great vacations, and generally lived out my own personal version of the great American Dream.

I'm here today to let you in on a little secret. It's not a dream. It's a fantasy.

It is painful to admit to an audience of readers just how short-sighted you are, but if I don't tell you the truth, you probably won't grasp just how bad things were before I started to turn things around. So here is the unvarnished truth:

I bought as much house as the banks would allow me to buy.

I took out the absolute maximum amount I could borrow to buy the best car my lender said I could afford.

I upped my credit limits at every turn to buy new electronics, new clothes and take fancy vacations.

I paid the minimum payments only on my student loans so I had more cash for the 'things' that I thought were making me happy.

Every single dollar that came in went straight back out again. I paid my bills on time, and then spent every other red cent living the life that I was so sure that I'd earned.

Well, here's the cold hard truth: when you're living the high-life on credit, you haven't 'earned' any of it. In my story, it all came crashing down one day in early 2012.

Rock Bottom

It's a story that many Americans are familiar with. You get called into your boss's office and told that the economy simply isn't allowing the company to continue the way it once did. In the face of all that external economic pressure, the company is forced to make cutbacks, and the next thing you know, you're unemployed.

It all happened very, very fast after that. I had no savings to speak of, no emergency fund. Within three months I was forced to sell the house. The car was repossessed. My phone started ringing five, ten, twenty times a day as creditors tried to collect on my outstanding balances.

With no other options, I was forced to move in with my brother. The high-flying young executive was now 30 years old and sleeping on his brother's basement couch. When my phone would ring, I would immediately hide it from other's view so they wouldn't see that it was yet another creditor calling me. I would physically flinch when the phone rang, or when a letter came in the mail.

In short, I was embarrassed, humiliated, and defeated. Like us all, I've had some low points in my life, but this was the worst. For another few months, I would sit in my brother's basement on my laptop, (which I also still owed money on) surfing the job ads. Every single ad seemed wrong. I was over-qualified or under-qualified, or it wasn't enough money or prestige. And STILL I was in denial. I kept telling myself that it would turn around any day now, and I would be just fine.

I hit rock bottom on November 16th, 2012. I tell you this, because the date is one that I'll remember forever. I went into the grocery store and tried to buy my groceries for the week. My card was declined. So I tried another one: declined. My third and final card – declined. I didn't have enough cash in my wallet. As the line mounted behind me, I had to mumble my apologies and walk out of the store.

As I walked home, I suddenly realized that this was as bad as I was going to LET it get. I wasn't delusional, so I knew it could get worse. There were people out there who were homeless, who didn't have a brother who could or would take them in. I still had my clothes, my computer, and my education. For the first time since I was a kid, I think I really appreciated what I HAD, and on that walk home, I was determined to make the most of it.

Back to School

The next day, I went to the library. Now, I hadn't been to a library since my college days. In my 'old' mindset, people with money, with jobs, and with status bought their books. They certainly didn't borrow them. But I didn't have any of those things now. My ego was gone, deflated like a child's balloon. And I was determined to find some ways to refill it at the public library.

I checked out every book on job hunting, resume writing, financial management, budgeting, debt management and a half dozen other more obscure topics relating to the dilemma at hand. I had been a good student once, and it was time for me to be one again.

None of those books, methods, or tidbits of advice changed my life. None of them was a magic wand that made the job and money problems go away. But contained within them, was the information that I would need to start working my way out of the situation I'd put myself in.

I've thrown out what didn't work for me, tried to crystalize what did, and hopefully, have presented it here in a clear, easy to understand and easy to act upon format that will help you make some of the changes that have helped me completely turn my life around.

It's hard work. You won't wake up one morning and realize that your money problems are solved. But, if you put some of these pieces of advice into action in your own life, create a financial action plan for yourself, and stick to that plan, then something WILL happen. You'll wake up tomorrow, and your finances will be slightly better off than they were the day before. The day after that, they'll be a little better. The day after that, even better. And after weeks, months and years of hard work and dedication, you can achieve the financial goals you set for yourself, restore your financial well being, and never have to feel the way that I felt that day in the grocery store.

I don't know where you are in your personal financial journey. Maybe you've had your grocery store moment. Maybe your debt is mounting, and you're trying to nip it in the bud before it gets to that point. Maybe you're just aware that your spending, saving and budgeting habits aren't what they could be, and you're looking for a way to set yourself up better for the future.

Whatever your personal situation, I truly believe this book can help. Read the book, try the exercises, keep what works, throw away what doesn't. If you make a plan and stick to it, I promise that a year from now, your finances will look very different than they do today.

So, that's my story. Who I am, and what I went through led me to write this book. Its up to you to take what you will from it, and be the author of what happens next, in your story.

My True Calling

In reality, I now truly believe that hitting that rock bottom was the best thing that could have happened to me. I realized that I couldn't care less about high-finance and the business world. Instead, I found my calling in personal finance. I truly love helping everyday people find ways to better manage their money.

Ultimately, my life is more fulfilling, more rewarding, and more fun since I've made this change. I thank you for letting me be a part of your financial education, and hope that some of the personal financial ideas I've acquired along the way can help you in some small way.

Chapter 2

The Benefits of Money Management–Stopping the Madness

After my epiphany at the grocery store, I realized that I wasn't "too good" for all those jobs that I'd turned my nose up at in the want ads. The first thing I did after my trip to the library was rework my resume, turn down my ego, and go out and apply for as many jobs as I possibly could. Nothing was off limits, as I realized that having any amount of money coming in was better than the ZERO that had been coming the last few months.

It was about three weeks later when I got the call. I'd been offered a position. It just barely brushed up against my field and past experience, and was a much more junior position that paid about a third of what I had been making previously. And yet, I was more grateful for that opportunity than almost any that I had been given previously. Hunger truly is the best sauce.

Now that I had some money coming in, I needed to decide what to do with it. The key word in that sentence is "decide".

Conscious Thought Vs. Reactive Spending

Before this moment, I typically never gave money a second thought. It came into my account, and I spent it when and how I pleased. It doesn't matter how much money you make. If you don't think about your money, if you don't consciously decide what the best uses of it are, and most importantly if you don't create a PLAN for your money, then you will find it constantly slipping through your fingers.

This was brought into stark focus for me when I got my new job, because I had so much less money coming in than I was used to. This is when I started learning about budgeting.

Budgets: An Introduction

So, what is a budget? Essentially, it is a plan for your money. You'll read a lot of complicated explanations and descriptions of budgets in a lot of money-related books, but the truth is that a budget is simply a plan for your money. Once you know how much money you have coming in, you make a plan for how you will spend, invest or save it.

We'll get to the nitty-gritty of how to put together a budget and how to make budgeting simple in the later chapters, but for now, let's look at WHY budgeting your money is so important.

First of all, knowledge is power. That might be a bit of an old chestnut, but it's the truth, especially when it comes to money. The problem is that so many of us don't know where our money goes. It's the problem of the "latte generation", where people just keep spending $5, $10, or $20 on the incidental little purchases of day-to-day life. When you're not even aware of how or where you're spending your money, how can you possibly expect to control it?

Creating a budget gives you knowledge. It lets you clearly articulate how much money you have coming in, and where it is going out. This immediately puts control of your finances back in your hands. Maybe, if you're like me, this will be the first time in your life that you're really in control of your own money.

Basic Benefits of Budgeting

There are many benefits to learning to manage your money properly. For me, the top 5 were:

1.   Regaining a Sense of Control

2.   Strategically Coping With Debt

3.   Being Able to Build a Savings Plan

4.   Capping Impulse Spending

5.   Focussed Goal Achievement

Regaining Control

When my great collapse began, it was essentially because I felt like I had no control over my finances whatsoever. I had no real sense of how much things were costing me. This was especially true when it came to interest – I had no IDEA how much interest was accumulating on my debt each month when I was only making minimum payments on my balances.

When you've got a budget, and when you're actively managing your money, suddenly, you're in control of everything. You're in control of how fast your debt gets paid off. You're in control of your house, your car, your credit rating and how fast you can achieve your goals. When you've suffered a job loss or financial distress, the sense of empowerment that you can regain by taking ACTIVE control of your financial well being is worth a great deal.

Strategically Coping With Debt

Debt is a reality for almost everyone living in this country. Unless you're in that elite 1% that doesn't need to borrow a cent, chances are you're in debt to someone. There are many different kinds of debt, and we'll get into that in a little more detail later on, but essentially there are "good debts" and "bad debts". All debt, whether or good or bad, needs to be managed.

By creating a budget and actively managing your money, you can come up with strategies to cope with debt actively, and create a plan for paying it off as soon as possible. Even if you have to live with "good debt" you can create plans for minimizing the interest that you pay. Interest is one of the absolute most insidious ways that our money disappears, and we'll look at a lot of different ways to minimize its impact in our lives.

A Savings Plan

This is a BIG ONE. When I was rolling high in what I sometimes call my "previous life" I didn't have a savings plan. In truth, I didn't even have a savings account. I just let all the money pile up in my account and then spent it. Most days I couldn't even have told you how much was in there.

Savings is a critical component of financial well being, and it doesn't have to be a horrible burden. By getting strategic and creating a plan, you can make saving so painless that you barely notice it. However, you can also make it EFFECTIVE, so that you will be quietly growing your nest egg every single day of the year.

Capping Impulse Spending

We live in a world where impulse spending is encourage everywhere we turn. In fact, impulse spending is so much more dangerous now than it was even ten years ago.

Think of all the ways you can spend money without thinking about it.

- You grab a coffee from a high-end coffee store on your way to work: $6

- You click a button on your phone to buy an app: $5

- You grab the magazine stacked by the till: $5

- You 'upsize' your meal at a fast food restaurant: $2

- You purchase a snack while at a sporting event: $8

- You buy a lottery ticket in passing: $5

- You grab lunch instead of going home or eating your packed lunch: $15

There are many people who will do several of these EVERY SINGLE DAY. I was certainly one of them. Looking back on my statements from the months before I lost my job, I can see that there were many days where I spent as much as $25 on impulse purchases alone.

Imagine that projected over the long term. That's $175 per week. Even scarier, that's $750 per month! That's what some people pay in rent! Or, to truly see how bad this is, you could project that kind of spending over an entire year.

The result is that you would have spent $9125 dollars on impulse purchases. There are many high-quality used cars you could buy for that much money. Obviously this is an extreme projection, and in most cases it isn't really this bad. However, imagine even having an extra $3000 or $2000 in your bank account at the end of the year. Would you trade a few lattes and other impulse purchases for that money? I sure would. And did. And my life has never been better.

Goal Achievement

Some people think that managing your money, creating a budget, and saving means that you'll never get to have any fun with your money. I've discovered that it is the exact opposite. In fact, it is GREAT to have goals for fun things that you want to do with your money, like taking a vacation or buying that new TV.

The difference is that this way, you'll actually get to enjoy what you buy when you reach your goals! I bought many of the things I thought I wanted, and systematically had them taken away because they weren't really mine! They belonged to the bank, or the credit card company, or the store, and after I lost my job, I had no means to pay for them.

When you set a goal as part of a money management strategy, you will slowly put money away until you can achieve one of your goals, like taking that trip to Disneyland with your family. The best part is, when you achieve it, you won't pay for it on credit, you won't pay interest on the trip, and you'll be able to really, truly enjoy it, because you will have worked hard to save up and achieve the goal.

Ultimate Benefit: MORE Money

Really, if you skipped the whole chapter and jumped to this section, I hope that it would be enough to convince you to start actively budgeting and managing your money. The number one reason to create a budget, is that if you do it, you will ultimately have MORE MONEY. You'll have more money by the end of the first month that you put it into action, and more importantly, for the rest of your life.

There are probably millions of people in this country alone who have less money than they could, simply because they haven't taken a proactive approach to financial health. They let it slip through their fingers, pay outrageous interest and fees, and never put their money to work for them.

By taking even a few of the steps outlined in this book and putting them into practice, you CAN HAVE more money, without needing to earn any more, because you'll be making the best use of what resources you have.

Of course, if you CAN earn a little more, even better, and we'll have some tips on that later on in the book!

Chapter 3

The Real World Value of Budgeting and Saving

Budgeting and saving go hand in hand. Let's face it, saving money isn't the sexiest thing in the world. It is way more fun in any given moment to go out and buy that fancy dinner and drinks for your friends than it is to squirrel that money away as an investment somewhere. But in reality, saving is going to lead to more pleasure and less pain as life goes on. It just doesn't provide you with that instant gratification, which is something that we'll get into in the next chapter.

In reality though, while saving isn't sexy, having a lot of money really IS. The sense of achievement, confidence, and wellbeing that comes with knowing that you're financially secure is unmatched by all the short-term highs I got by spending my money on the things I wanted. If you REALLY want to live "the life" you have to work at it by saving and planning, NOT by whipping out the credit card every time you spot something that you think you want.

Budgeting and Saving – Two Sides of a Coin

Most people think of budgeting and saving as two different exercises. Budgets make them think of spreadsheets and calculators, which is a method that works for many people, and saving calls to mind ideas of retirement funds, savings accounts or investments.

But in truth, for most people, saving and budgeting go hand in hand. Because without applying at least a little bit of budgeting to your income, saving becomes all but impossible.

For most of us, saving is the last thing we think about doing with our money each and every payday. This is partly because we live in a world where the cost of living is increasing much faster than our salaries. But it is also because we've been taught and trained that happiness lies in "bigger and better."

What do I mean by this? I mean that advertising companies, retailers, and especially the credit card companies have taught us, that if we want to be happy, we need a bigger house, a faster car, and a more exotic vacation.

I will tell you something that I know from personal experience. The feelings you get from a well managed, growing, and secure investment portfolio, FAR outstrip any temporary feelings you might get from buying a bigger house than your friends.

By creating a budget and making savings a priority, you're setting yourself for a lifetime of success and happiness. You can't get that by walking out and buying something you can't afford. It just isn't sustainable.

The Safety Net of Savings

This list isn't intended to frighten you, merely to call to mind just how important having savings is.

Here are 10 things that could go happen, any day, to any person. Each one of them could cause an expense that you haven't planned for. For many of us, this results in having to borrow money just to get through our daily lives.

1. Unexpected mechanical failure on a car

2. Damage to your house that isn't covered by insurance

3. Uninsured medical expenses

4. Sudden need to travel (family, work opportunity, etc.)

5. Uninsured dental issues

6. Job loss

7. Illness of a loved one

8. Pet illness

9. Natural disaster

10. 10. Computer Failure

Now, these events are awful anytime they happen, there is no doubt about that. However, think about how much worse they are (hopefully you've never been there, but many of us have) if you absolutely have no way to pay for them. If your accounts are empty, your credit exhausted, and if you don't have friends or family to borrow from, you could find yourself in a very serious situation if you don't have the means to pay for just ONE of these expenses, and I know people who have experienced many of them all at once.

With a proper budget and savings plan, you can find ways to tuck away money every time you have income coming into your possession. This helps you create a buffer between you and these types of events, so when (notice I didn't say IF – the unexpected happens to everyone) something like this happens to you, you just dip into your savings, deal with it, and move on with life.

This also brings you incredible piece of mind. When I hit rock bottom, I lived in absolute dread of the unexpected. I knew that if something happened, I was woefully unprepared to deal with it. Living in constant fear and stress is no way to enjoy life, and the comfort that comes from having that savings cushion can't be overestimated.

Saving money can play many different roles in your life. However, the most important one is that it gives you the tools to deal with all the little problems that crop up when "Murphy's Law" decides to rear its ugly head. Whatever can go wrong, eventually will, but if you have some savings, you can face problems with confidence.

Retirement

This is the other BIG reason why budgeting and saving is so important. If you continue to live pay check to pay check your entire life, what happens on the day that you are no longer able to earn one? That aside, don't you want to escape the grind some day, and enjoy your golden years?

We've all seen people who haven't been able to achieve this. There are many people who are well over 65 working minimum wage jobs. Its true, some of them do it because they like to stay active and to feel useful, and that's great. But, there are also many people in their late sixties, seventies, and even eighties, working minimum wage jobs because they've been forced into retirement by their lifetime careers, and have no means to support themselves now that their first career is over.

Like it or not, being advanced in years can make it difficult to find employment in many fields, and so many of them find themselves working jobs that in a past generation were reserved for teenagers getting their first tastes of employment. Entry level retail, fast food counters and even entry level factory jobs are increasingly being staffed by seniors who need an income just to survive.

If you want to avoid this, you need to start saving for retirement. There are three key concepts at play in making this happen, and they each relate to each other.

1. You must create a budget that reserves a certain amount each month to be set aside in your retirement fund. (which can take many forms, and in fact, should be diversified, but more on that later)

2. You must find ways to make your money work for you. Compound interest is your best friend when it comes to retirement savings.

3. You need to start as early as possible. It doesn't matter if you're 20, 30, 0r 40, whenever you're reading this book, if you haven't started saving for retirement, the time to start is when your next pay check comes in.

What is Compound Interest?

Now, if you've ever read any other book on managing your money, you've probably been introduced to the concept of compound interest. If you have, then this will be going over old material, but it is important to include this concept for anyone who isn't familiar with it.

Why?

Because, simply put, compound interest is the single most important concept to grasp when understanding why saving and budgeting is important.

It's that big of a deal.

Let's try and get a handle on just why compound interest is so important.

Imagine, that you are going to save a total of $100,000. This is just a sample number that I've picked for ease of calculations; it's not some magic bullet that you need to shoot for. For now, let's say that $100,000 is the amount that you will contribute to your own retirement accounts over time.

Now, let's say that you start investing when you're 20, and are going to put money away every year until you're 60. That's 40 years, or 480 months. That means that to put away close to $100,000 you'd have to invest approximately $208 per month.

This is where the power of compound interest comes into play.

Compound interest is what happens when your investment grows over time, with the interest being added to the principle rather than being withdrawn. Not only do you earn interest on the amount that you put into the account, you also earn it on the interest you've already earned? Make sense? Not yet?

Okay, let's round that investment number down to $200 per month to make this easier again. When you invest $200 and earn 6%, that breaks down to .5 percent per month. That means that in the first month, you'll earn $1 in interest.

Now, that doesn't sound like much. Except that in month 2, you'll earn interest on $201, not $200. On top of that, you'll save another $200, so your principle will have grown to $401.

Here is a sample progression to demonstrate the power of compound interest. We're going to break down exactly what happens to your money thanks to monthly compounding, over the course of a year. This assumes that you're putting away $200 into this account each month.

Monthly Balance	Interest Earned	New Balance
Month 2: $401	$2.01	$403.01
Month 3: $603.01	$3.02	$606.03
Month 4: $806.03	$4.03	$810.06
Month 5: $1010.06	$5.05	$1015.11
Month 6: $1215.11	$6.08	$1221.19
Month 7: $1421.19	$7.11	$1428.30
Month 8: $1628.30	$8.14	$1636.44

Month 9: $1836.44	$9.18	$1845.62
Month 10: $2045.62	$10.23	$2055.85
Month 11: $2255.85	$11.28	$2267.13
Month 12: $2467.13	$12.34	$2479.47

Now, since we deposited a total of $2400, we earned (roughly) $79.47 in interest, thanks to compounding. Now, this might not seem like much at first, but it's what happens over the long term that makes this so magical.

Say you keep investing that $200 a year for 40 years at 6%. By the end of that term, you've invested $96,000. Except that the actual amount of money you will have in your account will be closer to $400,289.64. That's more than $300,000 that you will have made for doing nothing more complicated than putting away $200 each month into the right investments.

That is the real power of compound interest. It might not look like much when you look at the year-long model. But when you project it over decades instead of years, it becomes clear that you don't have put away huge amounts of money to set yourself up to be extremely comfortable in retirement. All it takes is consistency.

Having a Plan

While compound interest is the best monetary reason to save and budget, I find that the comfort of a PLAN is the best personal reason to do so. Not having a plan is all well and good when everything is going perfect, but life isn't perfect 100% of the time. If you've got a plan though, you're read to deal with all the little ups and downs that life might deal your way.

So, next, we're going to look at just why this type of planning is so difficult for so many people, and then, we're going to look at how to overcome that and start learning about the nuts and bolts of budgeting and saving.

Remember, your plan doesn't always have to stay the same. Creating a budget isn't about locking yourself in stone. There are hundreds of things that can change your budget, including your marital status, your job, or your goals.

However, if you've got a plan, and have gotten used to employing a plan when it comes to your money, you'll find that it is easy to adapt to new situations. In fact, that plan will make you much more flexible than simply flying by the seat of your pants ever could.

Chapter 4

Why Managing Money
Can Be Difficult

Now, if there was one blanket answer to this question, the person who came up with it would instantly become a millionaire. The truth is that there are many reasons why people have difficulties managing their money. For some people, one of these reasons has an overpowering impact on their life. For most people though, these factors interact in combination with each other, and with many other factors that are unique to each person's situation. The result is a situation where a person has a difficult time managing his or her money.

These reasons aren't listed in any particular order. Each one is a factor that I have seen in myself, or in others, that prevents them from managing their money as well as they could. My hope is that by recognizing these factors in yourself, you'll be able to start taking action to keep these things in check when we move on to actually putting our budgets together, and more importantly, when we start trying to put them into action!

Instant Gratification

This is a big one, and it was one of the biggest problems that I had when it came to managing my money before my own personal crash. We live in a society where everything has sped up. The Internet, our cell phones, and the speed at which information travels means that we want everything right now. We have a deep-seated psychological need for instant gratification. The problem is that when we use our money to satisfy that need, it gets us in to trouble more often than not.

This is one of the largest factors that led to my hasty spending, and I'm sure some of you are nodding your heads right now too! On some level, I always knew that putting money away was smarter than spending it "right now". But that seemed like such an academic exercise to me. On the other hand, if I went out and bought something I wanted right this instant, I would get that instant flush of satisfaction that comes with buying yourself a new toy.

Shopper's High

There is actually a psychological mechanism at play here that you may or may not recognize. Some psychologists talk about an effect known as "Shopper's High", which is the great feeling you get when you buy yourself things. When you shop, especially for new things, your brain actually releases dopamine, which is the same chemical that is triggered when you have sex, or eat delicious food. More dopamine is released when something is new, which is part of why it can be so hard to control impulsive purchasing behaviour.

However, we live in a world where we need to learn to control a wide variety of impulses, and learning to control this one is just as important. By doing so, not only do we save money, but also we actually deny ourselves a little pleasure now for a great deal more pleasure down the road. Because believe me, having a large nest-egg in the bank waiting for retirement, and living the life you want to live, is a LOT more pleasurable than dodging telephone calls from your creditors.

Training ourselves to avoid that shopper's high, and to focus on our long-term goals is a big part of what managing money is about. Budgeting and saving isn't about denying yourself the things that you want. It is about making sure you can actually have the things you want over the long-term, instead of rushing in for that short term burst of pleasure, only to be denied everything else in life later.

Lack of Organization and Awareness

This is another big one, and one that we really have no excuse for anymore, given the technology that we now have at our fingertips. In an upcoming chapter, we'll look at all the ways that you can use technology to make organization easy and painless.

Many of us though, suffer from a chronic lack of organization in our financial lives. As I already mentioned, I barely knew how much money was in my bank account most days before I lost my job.

Although technology can provide the answer to this problem, it is also part of what caused it. When you used to get a physical pay check and have to go to a bank and cash it, it caused you to be very conscious about the money going into your account. The same went for spending cash in your wallet. You had a very visual reminder of just how much money you'd spent in a given period.

However, in the days of direct deposit and credit and debit cards, many of us don't give these things the kind of thought that perhaps we should. I know in my case, I simply used my credit card to pay for everything, and then at the end of the month did an online transfer to pay it down (often for not much more than the minimum payment.)

When you live like this, you have no real ongoing awareness of what kind of shape your finances are in. It's impossible to know how to make the right decisions and to save and strategize if you don't even know where you're at currently!

Lack of organization is especially present when it comes to our spending. Either we don't track it at all, or we hold on to our receipts in a giant pile for tax season. This lack of organization and awareness means that we have no real idea of what we're spending, or where we're spending it.

In the chapter on technology, I'll talk about some budgeting apps, as well as some for tracking your spending. Even if you're not inspired to create a full budget after reading this book, I hope you'll try tracking your spending using one of these options. It really provides you with a crystal clear picture of where your money is going. The organization into categories can also help you build your budget by tracking your spending for a few months in order to see trends and patterns that might dictate where you should be spending less.

Intimidation

Many people are intimidated by the thought of having to manage their own money. They think budgets are complicated or time consuming, and that saving and investing are either esoteric or akin to playing the lottery. None of this could be farther from the truth.

Education is the best counter to this intimidation. If you use the tools in this book to fill in any gaps in your knowledge, you will have less and less reason to be intimidated by the prospect of taking control of your finances.

Remember to use this book as a jumping off point. I don't pretend to have all the answers here! What I do have is a lot of good information that I have tested and put to work in my own life. This is what works for me, but you might find that you still have more questions. I want to encourage you to do what I did when I was working my way through the financial books that helped me dig my way out of the mess I had gotten myself into.

Keep notes as you're working your way through this book. Most importantly, write down any questions you might have. If I give you some information about mutual funds for example, but you have more questions or want to learn more about that topic in depth, then write down all the questions that occur to you. By making yourself proactive about improving your own financial education, you can get comfortable with the topics at hand, and completely get over any intimidation you may have once felt.

The thing about managing your money is that there is a nearly endless amount of information available on the subject. It would be simply impossible to pour it all into one book. However, if you use this book to start creating your money management strategy, and to inspire you as to where you should turn your eye next for further education, then you'll be off to a fantastic start.

Blind Spending

I've already touched on this a bit, but it is such a large factor in why people have difficulty managing their money, that it is worth touching on again.

We live in an age where technology allows us to spend blindly. Credit cards mean that you can purchase almost anything without ever having to watch money leave your wallet. This creates a sort of psychological bubble that insulates you from the true gravity of what you might be doing. This problem is especially an issue among young people, and something that really needs to be curbed before the personal debt crisis gets worse than it already is.

If I could only give you one piece of advise, it would be KEEP THE CREDIT CARD IN YOUR PANTS.

Credit cards ARE important. You SHOULD have one. However, you should have it for the following reasons:

- To provide credit in the case of an extreme emergency

- To help you book hotel rooms, rent cars, or reserve travel

- To help build your credit rating

Honestly, that's about it. There are many other reasons that some people will put forward about the benefits of credit cards, but I like to keep it simple. They're for the above purposes NOT for paying your bills or going on shopping sprees. They're a tool with a specific purpose, but we've started to look at them as "free money". Believe me, the reality is that credit cards are as far from free as it gets.

So, leave the card at home, or in your pants. If you do, you'll find it much easier to start managing your money effectively.

Chapter 5

Budgeting
Bootcamp – The Basics

So, let's get down to the 1st, and what I think is the most important, of my steps to gaining control of your money. Money management starts with budgeting, and I'm going to teach you how to create a budget in 6 easy steps.

Why is a Budget So Important?

The rest of the steps to managing your money all rely on having a solid budget. In fact, most of them are contained WITHIN the confines of a good budget. Without one, it is very difficult to make accurate decisions about the other aspects of managing your money. Think about each of these examples:

- You pay off $1000 per month of your debt, but find yourself short at the end of each month and have to dip back into your credit to meet your expenses

- You pay off your debt at a rapid rate but then encounter a situation where you need to draw upon your reserves, but you haven't been saving any money

- You spend so much on rent each month that you don't have enough money left over to adequately deal with your debt or to make adequate contributions to your savings

- You successfully pay off all your debt and meet your obligations for 25 years. When retirement rolls around, you discover that you have only enough money to survive for a few years without working

This might only be four examples, but we could spend pages listing more. We know that debt, savings, housing, income, and other expenses are all important portions of a budget. However, you can't make good decisions about any of those aspects of money management without a firm budgetary foundation. With that said, let's dive right in!

Step 1. Calculate your Monthly Income

This is the foundation on which your entire budget will be built. Figure out how much money you have coming in from all sources. This includes things like:

- Salaried or hourly positions

- Tips

- Royalties

- Investment income

- Alimony

- Scholarships

- Rental income

- ANY other source of income

Sometimes calculating your monthly income is difficult if you're an irregular income earner. This could include if you work mostly on contract work, are a business owner or are self-employed. If this is the case, you have to operate a little differently when you're making a budget, but it is still possible.

I've actually included a brief chapter later on that looks at this issue. Your income might fluctuate, but there are some techniques that you can use to come up with a workable budget despite that.

These tools will give you a good starting point, but you certainly have to remain on top of the situation. If you notice that your income drops or increases to any significant degree, you have to adjust your budget accordingly. This is especially important if the change in income is more than a one-time anomaly.

We'll get into income further in the next chapter!

Step 2. Calculate Your Debts

This means calculating all of your debts, from all sources. There are two things that you should find out when gathering information about your debts. These are: the total amount of the debt, and the interest on that debt.

Debts can include:

- Mortgages

- Car loans

- Instalment loans

- Lines of credit

- Major credit cards

- Department store credit cards

- Student loans

- Personal loans

- Payday advances

There are many other types of loans and debts that you may have, but we'll go into more detail on that on the chapter on debt. However, I want to shout out one tip right now, before we go a step further.

AVOID PAYDAY LOANS AT ALL COSTS.

I can't say that enough. The interest rates and fees charged by these organizations border on the criminal, and in fact, there are wheels in motion in many locations that will further change how these organizations attempt to do business. However, the bottom line is, you should avoid them like the plague. Nothing could be more detrimental to your bottom line than succumbing to the marketing ploys of the payday advance firms.

Step 3. Calculate Your Fixed Expenses

This is a pretty straightforward portion of your budget. Essentially, you just need to itemize your predictable monthly expenses so that you can account for them out of your income. Examples of fixed expenses include:

- Mortgage or rent payments

- Electricity bill

- Heating bill

- Water bill

- Internet bill

- Phone bill

- Car loan or lease payment

- Day care payment

Yes, I realize that there is a little bit of overlap between the debt and the fixed expenses category. We'll cover that in the upcoming chapters, but for the purpose of a simple budget, you could consider a fixed expense as any payment that MUST be met on a monthly basis.

Step 4. Estimate Your Variable Expenses

This is one of the hardest parts of making a budget, but don't worry, we've got an entire chapter on it too! Essentially, this is where you make your most educated guesses as to how much money you need to spend ON AVERAGE, on fluctuating expenses. This includes things like:

- Food

- Entertainment

- Clothing

- Medical expenses

- Transportation

- Car repairs

And many, many other items. The exact list of variable expenses will depend largely on your lifestyle. For example, a pet owner has an entire category of variable expenses that a non-pet owner doesn't have to deal with.

Step 5. Plan for Savings

There are many different types of saving. There is saving for retirement, investing, building an emergency fund, and saving to achieve a certain goal. We'll cover all of these in our chapter on saving money, so suffice it to say for now that you need to decide how much you need to save, and include that in your monthly budget.

Step 6. Create Your Budget

This is the step where you put all the information together and see where you stand. There are many different ways to do this, and we'll get into that in the next chapters on budgeting. You can create a budget using a notebook and a pen, a spreadsheet, or one of the many simple to advanced software tools that exist for that purpose.

Essentially, you can view your budget as this:

Income must = (Fixed Expenses + Variable Expenses + Debt Repayment + Savings Contributions)

If you create a budget using that simple formula and find out that your income can't meet those obligations, you have a budget deficit. This means that you will be going further in debt or failing to meet obligations. Unfortunately, all too many of us have been through this, and know that it can have catastrophic results. From losing your home to destroying your credit rating, when it goes to far, a regular budget deficit is devastating.

On the other hand of the equation, you could have a surplus. This might mean that you've got money left over after meeting all your obligations. This might seem like good money management, but it might not be. This could indicate, for example, that you're not paying down your debt quickly enough, or failing to contribute enough to your savings.

In reality, what we're aiming for is a balanced budget. This is what happens when our expenses meet our income, and all of our needs and obligations are account for in a suitable fashion.

That might sound easy enough, and really, using some of the tools I mentioned it could in fact be incredibly easy. However, in order to make sure that you're making the most of your budgeting, we're going to go into a bit more detail on every aspect of your budget. I've written a chapter dedicated to every element that I mentioned in the above formula, and then we're going to come back around and look at creating a functional budget.

Before we dive in though, here is an example of a functional, simple budget. Imagine that Mark has a net monthly income of $3200. Here's an example of a balanced budget for Mark. This budget follows some of the rules that we'll get into later in the book.

Income: Expenses

3200Mortgage Payment: $950

2250Food: $500

1750Savings Contribution: $320

1430Debt Repayment: $175

1255Utilities: $250

1005Transportation: $200

905Clothing: $100

805Entertainment: $100

505Car Payment: $300

355Medical Expenses: $100

255Car Maintenance: $100

55Babysitting: $200

0Miscellaneous: $55

There is a nice, neat, balanced budget. Is it perfect? Absolutely not. There are lots of ways that Mark could improve this budget, and hopefully, by looking at some of the information in the next chapters, you'll be able to create a budget soon that would put this one to shame. The point here is simply to illustrate how simple it is to create your basic budget. You just need to know how much is coming in, how much needs to go out, and then create a plan for that money that makes good, logical sense.

Chapter 6

Ideas for Increasing Your Income

O ne of the most defeatist things I ever heard anyone say came out of the mouth of a good friend of mine. I had begun to dig myself out of the money pit I had created for my self, and she was asking my advice on how to start correcting her own money troubles.

I started going over the concept of budgeting with her. After hearing how it worked, she sighed, and looked completely deflated. She said:

"I don't make enough money to pay for all that. I guess its only going to get worse."

This left me dumbstruck. I realized that she had completely given up. But I had good news for her. Our income ISN'T fixed! There isn't some gigantic ledger in the sky that dictates the exact amount of money that we're going to earn for the rest of our days! There are literally HUNDREDS of ways that you can earn money. If you're having problems with your financial obligations, one of the best ways to address them is to start looking at ways that you can bring in some extra income.

Types of Income

First of all, there are many different types of income. We touched on those in the last chapter. To recap, the ones we mentioned were:

- Salaried or hourly positions

- Tips

- Royalties

- Investment income

- Alimony

- Scholarships

- Rental income

- ANY other source of income

Now, these are pretty broad categories. As I've mentioned, one of the best ways to start solving, if not curing, your money problems, is to find ways that you can bring a little extra cash into your bank account.

So, I've complied a list of ideas that could help you earn a little extra money. These won't all apply to you, and many of you may find that only a few are actually practical given your unique set of circumstances. However, I urge you to explore those few, and see if you can start growing towards your real earning potential, instead of staying stuck in whatever income bracket you're currently in.

Remember, it doesn't take a lot of extra income to really change your situation. For instance, if you earned just $100 extra per month, but applied that amount directly towards whatever debt you have, you could find yourself debt free YEARS earlier than you might if you were only making the minimum payments on the balances that you owe.

Also, remember that this list is only the tip of the iceberg. Some might seem obvious, but they're REALLY only obvious if you're already doing them. Now, get out there and start earning!

Ideas for Extra Earning
(Ideas for Hourly or Salaried Employees)

1. **Get a Second Job.** – Many of us, especially those of us in the corporate world, think that we're too good, too important, or too educated for a second job. I'll tell you something. If you're in money trouble, you're not. Start applying for a night or weekend job to supplement your income. Millions of people work more than 40 hours a week, and you can too.

2. **Ask for a Promotion** – If you've already got a job, start thinking about ways that you can move up the ranks. Take on extra responsibility at every chance that offers itself. Talk to your superiors about training opportunities. Have a meeting about progression opportunities in the organization. Don't be afraid to just outright ASK if promotion opportunities are available. Often, advancement ends up going to those who express interest in it.

3. **Work Overtime** – If you're working an hourly job, again, this is something that can really help you dig out of that hole. Overtime pay is typically higher than your standard rate, and can add up quickly. Don't be too proud to ask

for overtime, and definitely jump on it whenever any opportunities for it come along.

4. **Earn extra credentials/train more:** There are many positions and careers where salary is based, at least in part, on the amount of certificates or training hours you possess. Jump on every training opportunity that comes along to try and push yourself into a higher pay bracket.

5. **Ask for a raise:** Again, this might seem simple, but you'd be amazed at how often it gets overlooked. I can promise you one thing: if you don't get proactive about getting raises, your employers probably aren't going to offer them to you unless they're mandated in your contract. Know what you're worth, and don't be afraid to go after it.

6. **Apply for higher paying jobs:** This one is a bit tricky, but in an economy like ours, it can't be ruled out. You have to look out for yourself, but you also don't want to be viewed as being disloyal. However, if you've asked for raises, overtime, and promotions and been denied at every turn, especially if you haven't had a path laid out for you as to how those things might be achieved in the future, then it is time to look at other options. Start putting out feelers for jobs that you might be well suited for that could push you

58

into a higher pay bracket. Reaching out to some recruiters to see what kinds of opportunities might fit your skill set can be a good idea here.

(Ideas for Commission Earners)

7. **Put in More Hours:** If you can get more hours on the floor, you stand a chance of increasing your commission.

8. **Negotiate a higher commission percentage:** Just like you have some ability to negotiate with your clients, your boss has some ability to negotiate with you, he just doesn't want you to know it.

9. **Take a second job in a different industry:** Commission jobs often contain a non-compete clause. For instance, if you're selling Hondas five days a week, you probably can't jump across town and sell Fords on a weekend. However, remember that good sales skills translate to almost any industry. You might not be able to sell Fords, but there is a good chance that your skills would make you an excellent furniture salesman.

10. **Network:** This can make your commission based earnings take a huge jump. By networking outside of your work

environment you can build a huge client base very quickly. Attend networking events, mixers, golf tournaments, chamber of commerce meetings and any other events where you might be able to make good connections with people that fit your buying demographic.

(Ideas for Royalty Earners)

Even if you're not at present a royalty earner, this can be a fantastic way to add some extra income into your pocket.

11. **Write a Book;** Even if you've never written anything before, this can be a great way to earn some extra income. You don't have to be the world's best writer, just honest and knowledgeable in some area. Write about what you know, and someone will want to read it. You can publish it through Amazon's platform and start earning royalties very quickly. If you're worried that your writing isn't of the most professional quality, use a freelance marketplace like Elance or Odesk to recruit an editor to give your draft a once-over before you publish it.

12. **Sell Photos:** There are many sites that sell photos and give a royalty to the photographer. A few to get you started are iStockPhoto.com, SmugMug.com and Alamy.com

13. **Sell Music:** If you've got a talent for music, record some short tunes and put them up for sale. The more you've got for sale, the more income you can get coming in.

(Ideas for Everyone)

14. **Work on a Freelance Market Place:** These marketplaces have needs for people with skillsets ranging from programming to writing to graphic design. Create a profile and start bidding on jobs in your area of expertise. ODesk, Elance, and Guru are good places to get started.

15. **Sell things:** If you've got a collection or other junk that you've accumulated over the years, start selling it. Niche sites and eBay are great ways to make profit over items just gathering dust.

16. **Resell things:** On the other hand, if you're an expert on comic books, used books, trading cards or anything else, you can try to buy them at a bargain locally and then resell them online for a profit. People have made small fortunes scouring garage sales and reselling collectibles online. You probably won't manage a fortune, but it can be an excellent

way to turn a fun morning of garage-sailing into a little bit of profit.

17. **Use Air BnB:** If you've got any extra room in your house, you can rent it out with this website to earn a little extra income. The site helps connect short-term renters with people with extra rooms or suites in their homes that they are looking to rent out.

18. **Teach:** Almost everyone has something worth teaching. Whatever your skill is, you can use your extra time to teach lessons on that topic. Ideas include musical instruments, foreign languages, tutoring in a given subject, etc.

19. **Consult:** On the other hand, if your knowledge is highly technical or specialized, for instance, if you have a law degree, engineering experience, or are an entrepreneur, you should look into offering yourself as a consultant to firms that might only need help with special projects rather than a full time other employee.

20. **Uber:** If you've got a car, consider signing up as an Uber driver to earn a few extra dollars.

21. **Fiverr:** Even if you really feel like you don't have the skills to work freelance, you can almost assuredly work on Fiverr, where people offer to do easy tasks for $5.

22. **Search Craiglist, Kijiji and other marketplaces for odd jobs:** Many people need help doing things like raking leaves in the autumn, or walking their dogs while they're on holiday. These classified websites are great resources for finding ways to earn extra money.

At the end of the day, absolutely anything you do to increase your income gives you more flexibility when it comes to creating your budget. For some, just one of these ideas might be enough to kick-start your earning. Others might have to go through every item on the list. At the end of the day though, it doesn't matter how you do it, only that you do.

Remember that ultimately you get out of life what you put into it. The same goes for your finances. If you've gotten yourself into a little bit of financial trouble, you're going to have to work hard to get yourself out of it. But, I promise you that the results are worth it.

Chapter 7

Understanding Debt

Debt is a pit that so many of us can get absolutely buried in. I know I've been there. Let's look at a couple of basic facts about debt to help us get educated, and then, I will give you some suggestions about how to handle debt when creating your budget.

Good Debt Vs. Bad Debt

These are terms that get thrown around a lot in financial circles. I use them too, because they're pretty commonly accepted when talking about personal debt. However, in my mind I tend to distinguish them as "tolerable debt" and "bad debt". No debt is great, but the right kind is certainly tolerable. However, it is so much better than the "bad" debts that are out there, that I don't mind calling it good!

There is a very clear-cut definition between good debt and bad debt when it comes to your finances. As far as I'm concerned, there are really only two types of tolerable debt: mortgage debt, and student debt.

For very advanced self money-managers, you could also have investment debt that could be considered good, but this is very risky and only for well-educated and skilled money managers. Typically this would take the form of a margin account, but it is definitely an area best left unexplored for the uninitiated. For now, let's assume that the only good debts are student loans and mortgages.

So why are these considered good? Well, there are two reasons. The first is that these are generally among the lowest interest debts that a person can have. The interest rates on both student loans and mortgages are currently many times lower than those on some "bad" debts like credit cards.

The other reason, and this is important, is that these are both a certain type of investment. When you pay for an education, even if you have to borrow money to do it, you are helping increase your future earning power. In the long run, you will come out on top here in most cases, even if you have to borrow money to do it.

The same goes for a home. When you purchase a home, you're not just paying for shelter the way you are when you're paying rent. You're also building equity. For many people, a house will be the largest single investment that they make during their lifetime. If the price of your home increases, or if you can rent part of it out, it becomes a real way to grow your money over time. Also, real estate is an important part of any diversified investment portfolio, even if the only real estate you buy is your own home.

However, this should come with a word of warning. There are MANY variables in the real estate market, and the topic of wisely purchasing real estate is so vast and complex that it would warrant an entire other book. What I will say on the matter is that real estate markets, interest rates, ongoing developments by the city you live in and a hundred other factors can affect the price of a property. So, don't simply rush out and buy a home because it has been classified here as "good" debt.

Instead, if you find that you're in a position to buy a house, start to do your homework. Like every other aspect of financial health, education is the key. Talk to some real estate professionals, do some independent reading, and then make an informed decision about whether or not purchasing a house is really the best financial move for you and your family. In many cases it may be, but there are also situations where it might be better to keep renting.

Bad Debt

This includes almost every other kind of debt. We're going to leave car debt out of this section for the moment, because it is sort of a special case that needs an independent look. One of the largest problems facing consumers today, especially young ones, is that amount of bad debt that they accumulate in a short period of time.

"Bad Debt" includes all high-interest and consumer debt. This includes credit cards, department store cards, lines of credit, personal loans and anything else that doesn't fall into the category of good debt.

Yes, I know that there are low interest credit cards and lines of credit out there. And yes, there are ways to use these responsibly. However, if you're reading a book on money management and are having problems with your financial situation, then you need to take a more simplistic look, at least until you get your finances under control. It is time to do away with bad debt as fast as possible.

Repaying Debt

When it comes to creating a debt repayment plan for your budget, there are a couple of things you need to consider, but one of the most important is the interest rates that you're paying on your debts. In most cases, you want to pay down the debt with the highest interest rate first. There are a few exceptions to this rule, but it is a good general principle to follow.

One notable exception is if you have one debt that has quite a low balance. If that is the case, you may choose to pay it off as quickly as possible to have a 0 balance and stop paying interest on that money altogether. That is not a bad strategy, as long as you can continue to meet the minimum payment obligations on your other debts.

Minimum Payments

This brings us to a very important point about minimum payments on debts. Whenever you have a loan or credit card, your monthly statement will let you know what the minimum amount you need to pay on the account is. However, there is a huge tendency by people to look at this "minimum" as "recommended". Believe me, this is NOT recommended.

If you make the minimum payment on a credit card with high interest, it might take you the rest of your natural life to pay off that debt. Let's look at an example.

Say you have a $7000 credit card balance at 19% interest. A typical minimum payment would be interest+1%. We can use the simulators at Bankrate.com (which is full of other great financial tools) to see how long it would take us to pay off that debt under that model. That would result in a minimum monthly payment of $180.83.

The unfortunate news is, that it would take 309 months to pay off that single credit card if all you made was your minimum payments. That's just under 26 years. To add some insult to that injury, you would also pay more than $10,000 in interest over that timeline.

Using that same Bankrate.com calculator, let's take a look at what happens if we up our minimum payment. Say we decide we can spend an extra $75 on credit card debt monthly. That would make our payment $255.83 per month. When you plug this into the calculator the results are SHOCKINGLY differently.

Under this model, it would take you 37 months to pay off your balance. That's just a little over 3 years. In addition, you would only pay $2246.99 in interest. So, you've just saved yourself 23 years of payments, and nearly eight grand in interest. Seems worth it, doesn't it?

That is just how insidious, tricky, and dangerous making the minimum monthly payment can be. The credit card companies WANT you to do this, as it means a huge amount of profit for them. You can beat them at their own game by making as much of a payment as you're able to in order to shrink your debt in a fraction of the time.

To run the simulation on your own credit cards, go to this link:

http://www.bankrate.com/calculators/managing-debt/minimum-payment-calculator.aspx?MSA=

and find out how much faster you could be paying off your debt!

Remember, this doesn't just apply to credit card debt. ANY debt where you're paying interest could really benefit from larger-than-minimum payments. When you get a mortgage or a car loan, one of the terms it is good to look into is the ability to make extra payments. Doing so can reduce the term of the loan, and the amount of interest that you pay over its life.

Car Debt

Car debt is a tricky subject, because there are a lot of misconceptions about car loans, and the value of owning a car.

Let me start by saying this. A car is a LIABILITY NOT AN ASSET.

That is perhaps the greatest single misconception that people have about buying a car. They assume that borrowing a bunch of money to purchase a car means that they're making an investment, and that they'll have something of value by the time they've paid the loan off.

This is true, in the abstract. But not at all true when you take the total picture of car ownership into consideration.

Cars are essentially money sinks. They require licensing and insurance, gas, oil changes, repairs and maintenance, fuel, tires and many, many other things. When you add all that on top of the interest that you're going to pay on a car loan, you will almost never come out on top. I say ALMOST because there are a few rare exceptions, such as investing in a classic sports car, where something may appreciate in value. But that is only a good idea for experts who have money to risk, not for someone trying to purchase reliable transportation.

So, am I saying to not buy a car? Absolutely not. I understand that for many people, purchasing a car is an important part of their life, and that they may absolutely NEED a car for commuting to work, shuttling children around and many other things. All I'm saying is that you need to recognize it for the liability that it is, and to be smart when paying for a car, especially when you're trying to improve your financial situation.

First of all, you should avoid purchasing a new car unless you've got money to burn. The depreciation that happens when you drive a new car off the lot is so severe that it makes it a poor bargain unless you absolutely can 100% afford it.

I prefer to buy a car that is a year or two old. This way, the car has already born the brunt of some of its depreciation, but still has some factory warranty left to protect me in the case of repairs.

You should also do some research into how fast a car depreciates before you buy it. If a car model plummets in value after a few years, it's not the greatest place to drop your hard earned money.

You should also consider the other costs of car ownership. Factors like the fuel mileage, reliability, and cost of licensing all affect how much it REALLY costs to own a car. To come up with a good figure, head to Edmunds.com and use their "True Cost to

Own" calculator. This let's you know what it REALLY costs to own and drive the car you're looking at.

It's also a good idea to do this to your current car. If you realize that the car is much more expensive to own than you realized, it can be worth selling it and re-investing in a more affordable or reliable model. Changing to a more practical car is a great way to save money while not sacrificing on lifestyle.

You can find the calculator here: _http://www.edmunds.com/tco. html_ and I encourage you to use it.

Also, remember to check the type of gas mileage that your car is getting periodically. An increase in gas mileage can have a huge affect on your monthly transportation costs. There are many things with a car that can go wrong that will affect your mileage, so it pays to just keep an eye on it from time to time.

Payday Loans and Cash Advances

I left this for last of the debt types because it is one of the most important things we're going to cover. We've previously discussed good debt and bad debt. Payday loan debt is not good, bad, tolerable or acceptable under ANY circumstances.

These places are, in my estimation, only one step shy of being criminal. The interest and fees that they charge make it almost impossible for a person to dig themselves out once they start down the slippery slope of utilizing their services. I hope that there comes a time in the future when these places are a thing of the past, but currently, they're a reality. However, they're a reality it is best for you to avoid.

Make no mistake, I UNDERSTAND that emergencies happen. I understand that life has a funny way of throwing a curveball at you when you least expect it. However, you need to do everything in your power to avoid going to these places.

Before you do, look into ways of making more money. Try to borrow money from friends or family members. Talk to your bank about the possibility of a line of credit. Although we would still consider this "bad" debt, it is certainly a better option than going to a Payday loan vendor if you're in an emergency situation and need some funds promptly. Even the most unfavourable terms on a bank line of credit won't come close to even approaching the interest on a Payday advance.

Budgeting for Debt

There need to be two big takeaways for you from this chapter. The first is that you need to find a way to budget to pay down more than the minimum monthly payments on your debts if at all possible.

The second is that there are different kinds of debt. No one expects you to pay down a 25-year mortgage in 5 years. (Although if you can make extra payments, great!). Instead, you need to focus on paying down your bad debt as quickly as possible. If you create your budget, meet your obligations, and have any money left over, where should it go?

Say it with me now....

Towards your DEBT.

Chapter 8

Fixed and Variable Expenses

Fixed expenses

Fixed expenses are the types of bills that you know you have to pay every month. Some people will group these in with what I call variable expenses, but I like to keep the two things separate.

Why?

Well, usually there are a lot less ways that you can lower your fixed expenses. Yes, you can do things to reduce your power and water usage, but these make a pretty negligible affect on your overall bill. On the other hand, the variable expenses we get to next are much more flexible, and we have more ability to play with them to save money.

Types of Fixed Expenses

These are those things that you absolutely must pay for, each and every month. Utilities often comprise a big portion of fixed expenses. Taxes may also be included in this category. Other common types of fixed expenses include:

- -Day care

- -Alimony payments

- -Health insurance

- -Car insurance

For the purpose of setting up your budget, you will also make your housing payments (mortgage or rent), your car payment, and any minimum payments on other debts part of your fixed expenses. You have to pay them every month, right? That's why they get included.

Now, there aren't a lot of ways to reduce fixed expenses, but here are 6 tips for reducing them every way you can. Anything you can do to cut back here will give you a little more flexibility when it comes time to budget for variable expenses.

1. **Bundle Services** – Many of us pay for cell phones, landlines, Internet and cable TV. If you're using a different

provider for each of these, you could be missing out on discounts that are available if you bundle all your services together with a single provider.

2. **Shop for better insurance rates:** Sticking with an insurer just because they're who you've used in the past is a terrible idea. You can use sites like Esurance.com to compare quotes from multiple companies to reduce your payments.

3. **Buy fans:** The amount of electricity it costs to run a fan is a fraction of what it costs to run air conditioning. Running AC throughout the summer is a sure way to wrack up a huge electric bill. Every chance you have to turn down the AC is a chance to save money.

4. **Improve home insulation:** If your home is leaking heat, you could be paying more to heat your home every month than you need to. Have someone come in and do an evaluation of where your home is leaking heat. A retrofit to insulate or seal it may cost money up front, but you'll save thousands in the long run.

5. **Cancel long distance plans:** Many of us pay for long distance phone plans that we no longer need. In the age

of VOIP, we can call our friends and family for free using tools like Skype or FaceTime over the Internet.

6. **Downgrade the Cable Package:** Streaming services like Netflix cost as little as 10% of the price of cable. Either cancel your cable or downgrade to the most basic package available and use Netflix or a similar service instead.

Variable Expenses

Variable expenses are those that fluctuate based on what you need in a given month. One of the most important uses of a budget is that it gives you guidelines for your various variable expenses. If you budget $100 for entertainment, once you reach that limit, guess what? No more entertainment for that month!

If you can stick to the discipline laid out by your budget, you'll be amazed how quickly your finances start to rearrange themselves in a positive fashion.

Here are 10 ways to reduce your variable expenses:

1. **Grow a garden, or join a community garden:** Gardening is a great way to lower expenses. First, it gets you exercise which keeps you healthy (which is a huge money saver, more on that later). Second, you can grow food for much

less than you would buy it. If you don't have your own garden space, join a community garden.

2. **Shop second hand:** Get it out of your head that second hand means "bad". You can find great things on Craigslist, Kijiji, eBay, or in your local thrift shop. Many are in like-new condition, but cost a fraction of the original price. This covers all types of items, ranging from furniture to clothing.

3. **Ditch the gym:** Gyms are all about prestige and marketing, not fitness. All it really takes to get fit is a pair of running shoes and the will to do so. Stop paying high monthly gym fees and start looking up ways to get fit using nothing more than your own body. To see what I'm talking about, visit *https://fitloop.co*.

4. **Take public transportation, walk or bike:** If you can arrange to take the bus or subway instead of putting more gas in the car, you'll watch your transportation budget consistently have a surplus. Walking or biking has the added benefit of getting you exercise minus the gym fees.

5. **Use Groupons:** Groupon and other similar services offer great deals on every type of product under the sun.

I have saved hundreds of dollars most months by using Groupons skilfully.

6. **Alternative entertainment:** Many of us spend WAY more on entertainment than we need to. Google "free activities" or "free entertainment" in your city, and you'll be amazed at how many options come up. You can also save a great deal by cooking at home and inviting company over rather than heading out to eat at a restaurant. The same goes for drinks bought and served at home compared to a bar.

7. **Comparison-shopping:** If you know you really need (or even want, occasionally) something, don't just buy it the minute you set eyes on it! There are apps and websites that will quickly scan all the stores that have a given item for sale and let you know where you can get the best deals. Pricegrabber.com is just one example of websites that can help you with this.

8. **Reduce Your Bank Fees:** The bank dings many of us every month with ATM fees, processing fees, and account fees. Talk to your bank about a low-fee account, or look into those offered by different institutions.

9. **Stop non-essential travel**: Yes, taking a vacation once in a while is a wonderful thing. However, you should be SAVING for vacations, not including them as part of your regular spending. Stick close to home while you resolve your money woes, and they'll resolve a lot faster!

10. **Buy in bulk:** Things like paper towels and tinfoil don't spoil, so buying them in bulk can be a great way to save money. Anything that won't go bad can usually be had for cheaper if you buy it in larger quantities.

BONUS TIP

Even though I said to ditch the gym, one of my BEST tips for saving money is to stay in shape. The body and the mind are connected, and you will never be at your best if you let your body get out of shape. Staying fit reduces your healthcare costs, will likely reduce your food and alcohol expenses, and will also allow you to work more. If you're tired and out of shape, it can be difficult to put in the hours you need to. Staying fit starts with the body, continues to the mind, and ends at your wallet!

Periodic Expenses

Not everyone allocates for periodic expenses in their budgets, and that's okay. By just adding a little more to savings for emergency use, you can be ready for these types of things. These include:

-Major car repairs

-Medical bills

-Unexpected home repairs

However, if you've got a good handle on the AVERAGE that these things might cost, you can allocate a small amount of money each month to a fund that will be designed to cover these expenses. For example, you could put $200 per month into a special emergency fund to cover these types of expenses when they arise. That would be a great way to be prepared to cover any of the eventualities that life can throw at you.

Chapter 9

Creating a Savings Strategy

T his is the most overlooked, and at the same time, probably the most important part of creating a budget. You absolutely, unequivocally, must start allocating some money to your savings right now.

I KNOW this can be difficult. I know it can be downright painful, especially when there are probably a hundred other things that you'd rather be doing with your money. But the truth is, that if you're not saving RIGHT NOW, then you're not going to be prepared when the next crisis hits.

I like to think of savings as several different categories. For me, these are chiefly

- Emergency Fund

- Goal based saving

- Investments

- Retirement Savings

We'll take a brief look at all of these in this chapter.

Emergency Fund

This is the most important of all the types of savings as I see them. This is the fund that will be there to cover your ass if your world falls apart. The reality is, this happens. It happens to me, and it could happen to you. If I had the emergency fund then that I had now, my life might have looked very different. But, then I wouldn't have learned the lessons that led me to write this book, and it would have been only a matter of time before I ended up back here anyway...

You'll read a lot of different views on how much you should have in your emergency fund. Usually, the least you'll hear is 3 months, and the most is a year. I prefer to split the difference and have a MINIMUM of six months funds in my emergency account.

This means, that you should have enough to cover every single expense that you would encounter over the course of six months. This means enough to keep paying your fixed expenses, your variable expenses, your debt repayments, and YES, even your savings contributions.

There is nothing to say that you shouldn't have MORE than six months in your emergency account. Its just fine to have a year's worth of money in there if you want. However, an emergency fund needs to be accessible to you. That means that you have to be able to get at the money right away should something come up. This makes a traditional savings account more suitable for it than an investment account or retirement fund. That is why I often like to leave mine right around the six month mark. I can take funds in excess of that amount and put them places where more interest and growth potential exists.

In my humble opinion, ALL of your savings should go into this account until you've built up a six-month buffer. Once you've done that, it is time to start dividing your savings up among the other options.

Also, don't forget: if you dip into your emergency fund, your new savings priority is to refuel it to capacity as SOON AS POSSIBLE.

Goal Based Savings

This is the type of savings that you do if you want to take a family vacation, or if you want to buy a new piece of furniture for your home. There is nothing inherently WRONG with this type of savings, however, you need to keep it within reasonable boundaries. In my mind, no more than 1-2% of your income should be going to this type of saving, and DEFINITELY none until your emergency fund is established.

However, goal-based savings can be one of the things that make it possible to stick to a budget. No one likes being told "no" all the time. If you deny yourself every single thing that you want, eventually you will throw your budget out the window, caution to the wind, and make those credit cards smoke all over again.

I know, because I've seen it happen.

However, if you have a goal-based savings plan, you KNOW that there is a light at the end of the tunnel where you will get something that you really want. I have seen this be the thing that helps people adhere to their budget, because they really want the reward that will come if they meet their goal.

And I will promise you one thing right now. When you save up for a family vacation and get to treat your family to that perfect trip, but you don't have to go into debt to do so, it is truly that much sweeter. You'll enjoy your holiday more, because there will be none of the stress or guilt that comes when you enjoy a luxury on credit. Instead, you can be proud that you were disciplined and earned that holiday!

Retirement Savings

Saving for retirement is another one of those topics like real estate that could easily make up a whole book on its own. Also, there is a great deal over overlap between "investment" income and "retirement" income, as you can use one or the other to achieve both goals.

The thing to note though is that you SHOULD be saving for retirement. You should make the maximum contribution to your retirement accounts that you can afford. A great trick is to take any raises that you get and have your employer immediately direct a percentage of them to your retirement account. You'll be used to living without the money and won't even miss it, yet you'll have taken a big step towards growing your nest egg for retirement.

Investment Income

Finally, there are those savings that you invest directly in a financial product. There are hundreds of options here, and there are two main types of investing: self-directed investing, and guided investing.

Neither of these is a better option than the other. However, if you plan on directing your own investments, be careful, and spend lots of time learning about various investments before you purchase them. There are a lot of risks and pitfalls out there. I'll give you a few of my favourite tips below, but take the time to go beyond what is offered here and learn as much as you can.

If you're using a financial advisor or planner to direct your investments instead of doing it yourself, the most important warning (and a common theme when it comes to investing) is to watch how they charge their fees.

Even if YOU don't make money, a financial planner or advisor has to. That's how they keep the lights on in their businesses. This means that you need to figure out how they assess their fees and how that affects any potential profit you might be making from your investments. There are unscrupulous investment professionals out there whose fees can essentially wipe out any profits you might have made with your investments.

Self-Directed Investing

Self-directed investing can be a lot of fun, and a great way to start building your wealth. However, it is a field that is full of landmines. Here are my top 10 tips for the new, self-directed investor.

1. **Beware of Mutual Funds:** Mutual funds seem like a great idea. They offer built in diversification and are managed by a professional. However, most mutual funds come with fees. A steep fee on a mutual fund can completely wipe out any return you might enjoy through the fund's growth. Unless you can find a 0-fee fund to get into, mutual funds are often best avoided by the beginning investor. However, they're heavily marketed towards those just starting out, so you really need to be aware of their drawbacks.

2. **Diversification is key:** You've probably heard this advice a lot when it comes to investing, but do you really know what it means? Diversification means holding a wide range of financial instruments, and having a wide range of specific products within those instruments. For instance, a balanced portfolio might contain stocks, bonds, real estate, and other instruments. However, each of those categories should also be diversified. For instance, your stocks should

contain many different companies from many different industries, to avoid being subjected to wild swings in any one area.

3. **Balance stability and risk:** You should hold a mix of low-risk, low reward investments that will help protect your balance, and some that hold a higher risk and higher potential for profit. For many people, this takes the form of bonds (typically stable) and stocks (typically more volatile).

4. **Look for low-fee brokerages:** There are now a wide variety of online discount brokerages that allow investors to buy and sell financial instruments for very low fees. This is a great way to save money when starting out.

5. **Build income:** Building some income from your investments is a smart move. It helps protect you when your other income fluctuates, and gives you more money to continue building your investment portfolio. Dividend paying stocks, DRIPS, and real estate are all examples of income options.

6. **Stay the course:** You've probably all heard of day trading, and heard legends of people who buy and sell several

stocks a day only to walk away with fortunes. The reality is that most people lose their shirts with a few clicks of a button. Day trading is the equivalent of playing poker – anyone with enough money to buy in can play. However, a very few, elite, skilled professionals who have spent years learning the game will typically take the money of every other amateur in the field. Buy investments to hold them and watch them grow, not in the hope of flipping them for a quick buck.

7. **Index funds are your friend:** Index funds are a very good place for the beginner investor to look towards. These have diversification built in, but you don't watch fees gobble up your profits the way most mutual funds do.

8. **Keep investing:** It's important that once you start investing that you stick to it. You can't just put money in for a few months and expect to grow rich. Investing is about continually saving more, increasing your diversification, and creating income over the long term.

9. **Start as soon as possible:** We talked about the power of compound interest earlier in this book. In all investing, starting early is the key to long-term success.

10. **Don't panic:** Markets fluctuate. This is inevitable. As a beginning investor, it is very easy to fly into a dead panic when you watch some of your hard earned money go up in smoke. However, you have to recognize that markets swing. This means they go down, but they also come up again. During the crash in 2008, many, many people panicked and sold in order to preserve what money they had left. Those people lost fortunes. On the other hand, those that stayed the course and enjoyed the rebound a few years later, made fortunes.

Savings in Your Budget

To really budget effectively, you need to budget for making contributions to your savings accounts. However, you should also strategize about where you're going to direct those savings.

Here are some guidelines for savings to incorporate into your budget:

- Your first savings goal should be your six-month emergency fund

- You should be saving at least 5% of your income. Once your debt is paid off, you need to be saving 10%.

- You should split your savings between account and investment types

- Put no more than 1-2% of your income into savings for "fun" goals

- Split your savings between traditional retirement instruments (IRA, 401K) and other investment options (like buying products through your discount brokerage)

Investing and saving is something that many people are scared away from. However, out of all the areas of money management, this is the one that it pays to learn the most about. I encourage you to read everything you can on the subject, because it is through wise investing and saving that you can set yourself up for a happy and comfortable future.

Chapter 10

Putting Together Your Budget Or Numbers, Numbers, Numbers

The time has come! It's time to create your first budget. For now, we're going to create a budget using a simple spreadsheet model. You can do this on paper, or in Excel or other spreadsheet program. This is just to teach you the basics of putting together your budget.

Once you learn these fundamentals, there are Much easier ways to incorporate budgeting into your daily life. I'll throw several ideas for this your way in the next chapter.

Step 1. Create Your Income Column

In the first column, list your income for the month. This should include the total amount (net) from all sources of income. We'll handle variable income in a later chapter, but for now, remember to aim low rather than high when estimating variable income.

For our example, we'll work with a sample net income of $3200 per month.

Income	
3200	

Step 2. Fixed Expenses

It's time to subtract our fixed expenses.

IMPORTANT – there are a number of rules that can help you understand WHAT your budget should be. If you exceed these rules, it might be a strong indicator that you're living beyond your means. One of the most important of these is the rule that indicates how much you should be spending on your housing costs. Ideally, no more than 35% of your housing income should be spent on your mortgage or rent payments.

In our example, this would be a maximum of $1120 per month. Now, as with any budgetary category, we're going to aim lower. So, in our example, let's say that the rent payment is $1000 per month. We enter this under "Housing" in the expenses column, and subtract it from our income. You don't have to inclue this, but for beginners, I like it as it keeps a running tally of your expenses as you're building your budget.

Income		Expenses	
3200		Housing	$1000
2200			

We've got $2200 left.

Now, we've got utilities. Since we're imagining a rental situation, we're going to count Internet, power, and a cell phone (our imaginary budgeter cancelled his cable to save money!) for a total of $180 per month.

Income		Expenses		
3200		Housing	$1000	
2200		Utilities	$180	
2020				

This leaves us with $2020. Our last fixed expense is going to be a car payment, fixed at $250 per month. We add this under expenses, and subtract it from our remaining income, leaving us $1770.

Income		Expenses	
3200		Housing	$1000
2200		Utilities	$180
2020		Car Payment	$250
1770			

We're just going to continue this process, using the items we've looked at in the previous chapters. For variable expenses, we'll estimate $400 for food, $500 for transportation and $100 for medical expenses. Add in another $150 for clothing and grooming. Now, we have $620 left.

Debt repayment is next. Our imaginary budgeter has a pretty sizable line of credit. The minimum payment is $95 per month, but we all know where that leads. We're going to bump that up to $150 per month to greatly speed up the debt repayment. $470 left.

We're going to aim high with the entire 10% for our savings, which will go directly into our emergency fund until it contains six months worth of income. In this case, that would be $19200. With $320 going to savings, we've only got $150 left.

It's okay to have a slight surplus. We'll allocate this to "miscellaneous" which can help cover all the little unexpected costs and hiccups that come up over the course of a month. If you get to your next payday and your surplus is still there, you should absolutely immediately send those funds to pay down your debts faster. If you're lucky enough to be debt free, put them into savings instead. At this point, the budget is going to look something like this:

Income		Expenses	
3200		Housing	$1000
2200		Utilities	$180
2020		Car Payment	$250
1770		Food	$400
1370		Transportation	$500
870		Medical	$100
770		Clothing and Grooming	$150
620		Debt Repayment (LOC)	$150
470		Savings	$320
$150		Miscellaneous	$150

Now we've created what is called the "Projected" part of our budget. In other words, we've created a plan for how much we should spend on each of our expenses in a perfect world. The next step is tracking how you match up to that plan!

Here, we're going to add "Projected", "Actual" and "Difference" columns to our spreadsheet. As you spend money throughout the month, you need to track it, and add it into the actual column. As you watch the difference between your projection and the actual change (you can set up a rule to do this automatically in Excel) you will see how close you are to your guidelines. If you're going over in one category, you NEED to cut back in another to keep your budget balanced!

Here is an example of a completed monthly budget. Here, we've got a slight surplus. Typically, I would either add this money to the emergency account, or roll it over into debt repayment once next month's income arrives.

Income	Expenses	Projected	Actual	Difference
3200	Housing	$1000	$1000	0
2200	Utilities	$180	$180	0
2020	Car Payment	$250	$250	0
1770	Food	$400	$375	$25
1370	Transportation	$500	$550	($50)
870	Medical	$100	$0	$100
770	Clothing and Grooming	$150	$100	$50
620	Debt Repayment (LOC)	$150	$150	
470	Savings	$320	$320	
$150	Miscellaneous	$150	$75	$75
			Total Difference:	$200

That's really all there is to creating a simple budget. It is nowhere nearly as complicated as you might have thought it was. Sticking to it however, can be more difficult!

You can make this as complex, or as simple as you want. A quick Google search will reveal dozens of pre-built Excel templates if you choose to use a spreadsheet to manage your budget. Color coding and fancy formatting can make it easier to read, but the basic concepts remain exactly as I've outlined them above.

One of the best ways to stick to your budget is to use some of the modern tools that are available for tracking your spending and budget. We'll review a few of them coming up.

Chapter 11

Budgeting Tools–Keep it Simple, Stupid!

Many of us have heard of the K.I.S.S. rules (Keep it Simple, Stupid!). This principle essentially tells us that we have a great tendency to overcomplicate things!

This certainly applies to the world of budgeting as well. I prefer to keep it simple. Technology has come so far, and now, most of us carry incredibly powerful computers around in our pockets. Using the technology available to us, we can make budgeting and budget tracking incredibly easy.

Also, many people in the past have given me the excuse that they don't make a budget because they don't have enough time. With the applications available for today's smartphones, that simply isn't an excuse anymore.

The following is just a rundown of a FEW of the products that are available to help you track your budgets. I wanted to give you a snapshot just to let you know what's out there, but there are dozens of other products that work very well on top of these. Don't be afraid to experiment, and once you find one that works for you, just stick with it.

Spreadsheets

The most basic budgeting tool is a spreadsheet. Using Microsoft Excel, you can create an easy spreadsheet with columns for your income and expenses. Itemize your expenses and you're off to the races.

You can also create rules that will automatically complete the calculations that tell you how your budget is balancing for the month.

Pros: Easy to Use

Automatic Calculation

Cons: Requires some spreadsheet knowledge

Requires manual inputting of expenditures

Not well adapted to mobile (mobile spreadsheet programs certainly exist, but they're not as intuitive or straightforward to use as some of the apps that exist.

Homebudget With Sync

Homebudget is budgeting and expense tracking software available for iPhone and Android. The best part about this is that it is very well suited to couples. You can have two phones sync together so that when one of you spends money in a certain category, it will update the budget that you're both using.

Pros: Syncing with other family phones

Intuitive interface

Manual adjustment of expenses

Cons: Paid app

Spendbook

Spendbook is another great option. The makers of the app pride themselves on having created an app that is actually enjoyable to use. Considering most people feel like budgeting is about one step above going to the dentist, that is a pretty high claim! However, it's clean interface and easily adjusted budgets do make it a pretty great option.

Pros: Notes and photos feature allows detailed tracking of expenses

Great interface

Low Price

Cons: No syncing between devices

Mint.com

Mint.com is a web service that also comes with an application that you can download to your smartphone. Mint actually synchronizes with your bank accounts, and COMPLETELY removes the effort of tracking and updating your spending. It even slots your spending into the appropriate categories so you can see how you're matching up with your budget.

Pros: Large support team

Almost universal account synchronization

Wide suite of features

Cons: Steep learning curve

Potentially overwhelming for beginners

Chapter 12

Budgeting Rules

Imentioned one of the budgeting "rules" a few chapters ago, when I said that most people place 35% as a hard ceiling on the amount that you should spend on housing costs. There are actually a number of rule sets that are useful when creating a budget.

These are for people who just can't make their income line up with their expenses. The reality in these situations is that you NEED to change your expenses. If that means downgrading your apartment, selling your car, or curtailing your entertainment spending, then so be it.

Any of these rules can work for you. The key, as I've said so many times, is to stick to the budget you create. You don't have to use these exact rule sets when creating a budget. Instead, you should look upon them as sort of general guidelines.

However, there is something to be aware of. If your budget doesn't come close to conforming to any of these budgets, that should be a red flag. These methods have been tested by sound financial minds, and are shown to provide people with a reasonable way of distributing their expenses. If you're not even close, it might mean that there is a problem within your budget.

The 50/30/20 rule

This is a simple rule that gives you very broad categories within to fit your expenses. Essentially, the rule goes like this:

50% of your income: Needs. This includes things like housing, your car payment, bills, and minimum credit card payments. Some flexible items come under needs as well, such as food and transportation costs, which you will have to estimate.

"30% of your income: Wants. Now, this is "wants" in the strict sense, meaning, you might consider them essential but you don't really need them to live. For instance, this might include non-work related travel, non-essential food, and meals out. Even the cable bill is a "want" when you really think about it.

20% of your income: Savings and debt repayment take up the last 20 percent of your income. How you allocate the funds within this portion will depend on your unique debt and savings picture at the present time.

The 25% Rule

This is another easy approach to budgeting. The difference with the 25% rule is that it utilizes your GROSS income rather than your net.

If you want to try this rule, the guidelines are as following:

25%–Taxes

25%–Housing

25%–Debts

25%–Living Expenses

This is a bit of a harsh picture, with a low percentage for housing and living expenses and a very strong debt repayment strategy. The giant flaw here is that there is no money allocated for savings. However, if you were in a severe debt crisis, an aggressive approach like this over the short term could have some applications. However, it is strongly recommended that as soon as you were able to, you switch over to a format that would account for some savings as well.

60/10/10/20

This is another percentile breakdown that uses broad categories but includes savings as not one but two of the categories. This plan could work very well for someone looking to increase his or her net worth over the long haul. This plan includes debt in the fixed costs however, and so requires you to have fairly manageable debt in order for it to be effective.

60%–Necessary costs – housing, transportation, debt, bills etc.

10%–Retirement savings instruments

10%–Savings – emergency fund, vacations etc.

20%–Wants – clothes, eating out, travel etc.

This is obviously a very liberal plan. In reality, it probably wouldn't work well for someone who is in a bad financial situation. However, if you use a plan with a stronger debt repayment element and then get yourself back on an even keel, this budget could work perfectly well for maintaining your finances into the future.

Chapter 13

The Battle Against Inconsistent Income

Irregular income is a fact of life for MANY people. Small business owners, consultants, freelance workers, contract workers, seasonal workers and people who live primarily off of royalty income may all have very variable income from month to month.

Obviously, up until this point in the book we've been dealing with fairly simple numbers when it comes to the "income" portion of a budget. You simply come up with how much money you earn, and work backwards through your expenses from there.

With irregular income earners, things are slightly more complex, but it's really not all that confusing. Irregular income workers often convince themselves that making a budget is actually going to be way more difficult than it is. In reality, you can create a budget no matter how much your income fluctuates; you just need to plan a little bit in order to account for that fluctuation.

Backwards Budgeting

One way to approach budgeting with an irregular income is to work your way backwards. In other words, you find out exactly how much you MUST have in order to make ends meet every month. Then, it is up to you to make sure you go out and earn that much each month.

This is simplistic, but can be effective. What you must do when applying this model is ensure that any excess money is put into your reserve fund. Also, when you're working with an irregular income, I HIGHLY recommend increasing the amount of your emergency fund to a year's worth of income rather than six months. This might take some time to accumulate, but the security you'll have once you've created that cushion for yourself is worth a great deal.

Minimum Income

Using the minimum income method, you create a budget by looking backwards over the past 12 months, and selecting the worst month of income that you had. For instance, if you made between $2500 and $4000 over the course of a year depending on the month, you will create your budget using the $2500 figure.

This might seem a bit severe, but it is a sure way to create a budget that you can live within. It can actually really give you a leg up in the long run, especially if you dump any extra money that you earn into savings or debt repayments. By using the worse case scenario as the basis for your budget, you give yourself a lot of wiggle room for the better months.

Average Cash Flow

This method is sometimes better if you have REALLY wild swings in your income from month to month. In this method, you calculate your 12-month average and use that as your income in the budget.

A word of warning with this method: it requires even more discipline than many other methods, because you will be forced to ACT as if you've earned your minimum, even if you've earned more.

For instance, if you have a widely swinging income, imagine that you earn $9000 one month. Your 12-month average was $4500. That doesn't mean you suddenly have $4500 of extra money. You have to save on to that, because there is a good chance that next month, you will only earn $2200, which would leave you with a big shortfall in your budget. However, as long as you roll the surplus over to cover your deficits (instead of spending it!) you should be just fine.

Repaying Your Savings

People with irregular income are much more likely than those with steady employment to have to dip into their savings. You need to train yourself to think of using your savings like a loan. Imagine that you're borrowing from yourself, rather than using money that is already yours. Then, you can create a repayment program (build it into your budget!) to repay the amount that you borrow from your savings in order to cover an especially lean month.

Rely on Cash

As we mentioned in the chapter on applications and budget tracking, using cash can be a very good way to keep track of how much you're spending in a given month. When you have irregular income, paying yourself in cash and then using it to cover your variable expenses is a very useful tool. That way, it prevents you from any of the easy over-spending that can occur when relying on plastic to make your purchases.

Prioritize

When you're on an irregular income, it is important to have set priorities for your expenses. This is because there may come months where you can't actually fulfill your entire budget. In this case, you need to know which needs must be met, and which wants can be left until the following month.

For example, you MUST pay your rent, credit card bills, and car payments on time. However, you may have an item in your budget for clothing. Unless you've experienced a disaster and suddenly lost all of your clothes, this is likely an item that can get pushed to another month.

This certainly isn't a lot of fun, and hopefully you can create a steady enough income stream to avoid it. The reality though, is that irregular income earners can be subjected to all kinds of fluctuations in their earnings to that make this kind of flexibility necessary.

Also, it is advisable to not borrow from your savings to cover things that you can really live without. You should only dip into that pool if you absolutely are falling short on something like rent, which you must pay for unless you want to face very serious consequences.

Chapter 14

Budgeting as a Team

Single people living alone have a fairly easy time when it comes to budgeting. You only have to worry about one income, and one person's set of expenses. The larger a family gets however, the more the complexity of a budget can grow. This doesn't mean that it has to be difficult however. You just need to take action when creating and implementing your budget to make it a family affair.

When creating a family budget, it is important that everyone is involved in the discussions from the outset when it comes to lying out the expenses. Even when a couple has been together a long time, one person may have very little idea of how much the other spends on certain items. Many serious relationship issues arise because of money, so it is best to start your discussions by being open and honest about what you have previously been spending, and what would be reasonable to spend going forward.

Creating a family budget and sticking to it means that you're going to need to have ongoing communication. You need to pick a means of creating and tracking your budget, and then you both have to agree to update it and keep it current so that you can ensure that you're following your budgeted guidelines.

This is where an app like HomeBudget can work very well. By automatically syncing your phones, it can ensure that both parties are on the same page financially.

If you prefer not to use that type of an app, you should set regular times when you can meet to talk about the family's finances and budget. Use this time to update the budget on a master document or spreadsheet so that you can see how you're doing as a team, rather than as individuals. Usually, I recommend meeting at least once a week to touch base to make sure that the budget is still on track.

I can't say this enough: a budget that you don't stick to is just numbers on a page! You need to actually adhere to the guidelines that you lay out in it for it to have any practical value. When you have two different people out there spending in all the categories, it can be very easy to get off track. That is why syncing apps or regular meetings are essential to keeping you focussed on your goals.

Family Cash Budgeting

The cash method can also work very well for families trying to stick to a budget. Withdraw the cash amount of each budget item and divide it amongst you as required. If you promise to leave the plastic at home, this forces everyone to stay within budgetary confines.

After you've been paid for the month, you should withdraw, in cash, the amount that you're planning to spend on all of your variable expenses. You can pay for your fixed expenses using a check or online banking, but everything else should be withdrawn in cash. Then, you can split the cash amongst the family members that take care of these purchases.

When you do this, you absolutely ensure that no one will go over budget, especially if you all promise each other to leave the plastic at home. This is a very simple way to keep on budget without having to even bother with weekly meetings or complex technological solutions.

Cash management was the ONLY way people had of managing their money for hundreds of years. The massive trend of consumer debt only happened after plastic became the preferred way of paying for things. I think about this often when talking to people about the money traps that are all around us in our present society. To my way of thinking, none of those traps is quite as insidious as the lure of using cards instead of cold, hard cash.

This can also be a great way to get the kids involved in budgeting activities, and to start teaching them about budgets and money. As parents, one of our most important obligations should be to pass some basic tenants of financial management along to our children.

There are a lot of kids out there in University or who have recently graduated who are in a lot of financial trouble. The credit card companies relentlessly pursue young people to try and gain their business, and the result has been generations of people with high-consumer debt and entry-level jobs: a sure recipe for disaster.

Get your kids involved early with the family budget to teach them the value of budgeting, saving, and sound financial management!

Goal Based Savings

This is something that it can actually be a lot of fun to work towards as a family. If you are saving for something for the whole family, such as a new TV, or a vacation, then making it a team activity is a way to keep everyone on budget, and to make the pursuit of the big reward very exciting!

One way to really involve people with this is to keep a running tally. Send out text messages to everyone in the family letting them know how close you're getting to the goal. You could also put the number up on the fridge or the whiteboard. By focussing on the fun part of the budget, it will help keep everyone focussed on adhering to the rest of it – because if they do, the reward will benefit everyone!

Chapter 15

Conclusion

I'm sorry if the subtitle of this chapter sounds a little bleak. I don't mean it to be! It is really my truest, most fervent wish that none of you have to end up with the level of financial ruin I found myself in.

That's why I wrote this book. That's why I work with people to help them create solid budgets that will keep their finances on track. Because I know how bad it can get.

I also know just how EASY it is to avoid this type of situation! It's not a full time job, hard work, or an exercise that requires a degree in economics. In realty, all it is is a little organization, a little dedication, and a little attention to the details. If you can manage that, you can straighten your finances around in a very reasonable amount of time.

I can't lie to you: it might be hard work. It might not be fun, at times. However, with the technology that you have available to you today, by involving your family to help support each other on the road to financial stability, and hopefully, with the tools in this book, it can be a very straightforward process that anyone can achieve.

I won't keep you much longer. I want to say thank you for reading this book, and for giving yourself the chance to avoid some of the mistakes that I made. If you put even a few of the ideas of this book into practice and stick with them, I think my wish will come true. I think you'll avoid ever seeing just how bad it can get.

And that puts a big smile on my face!

To make it even easier for you, I've wrapped the book up with a bonus chapter. This is a straightforward list of what I consider to be the 20 basic commandments of money management. If you want to cut straight through to the raw principles of keeping your money in order, I hope that this list will be helpful.

Thanks again. I hope the road ahead brings you happiness, and personal and financial well-being!

20 Commandments of Financial Well-Being

1. **Make a Budget:** It's the first, because I think it is the most important. You've got loads of tools in this book to help you make a simple budget. You can get as general or as specific as you want, but the very act of making and having a budget will make you get more deliberate and conscious about your finances, which is the first step to success.

2. **Use Technology:** It's all around us, and if you don't take advantage of it, you're missing out. Use Mint.com, budgeting apps, or spreadsheets. If you don't like any of those, use your smartphone's camera to take a picture of all your receipts so you are never in danger of losing track of your spending.

3. **Save Always:** Save a minimum of 5%, but preferably 10% of your monthly income. If you don't do this, you're doing

the future version of yourself a grave disservice, by denying yourself the benefits of long-term compound interest.

4. **Create an Emergency Account:** The best part of having a six-month stockpile of funds is that if an emergency happens, you won't turn to your 19% interest credit cards to bail yourself out. An emergency fund is essential for dealing with all the little twists and turns that life deals you.

5. **Save as a Family:** Creating a family savings goal is a way to get the whole team involved in responsible financial management. Without that, it can be very difficult, as it can feel like you're operating in a vacuum.

6. **Read More Financial Books:** Education is one of the most important weapons you have against financial ruin. Read books, including the classics like Rich Dad, Poor Dad, Think and Grow Rich, and anything by Warren Buffett. Each time you read, make notes, jot down questions, and let that spur you on to the next book.

7. **Manage Variable Expenses:** Many of us pay more than we need to for things, which is the equivalent of throwing money away. Find ways to reduce cable bills and insurance payments by comparison shopping.

8. **Negotiate Everything:** Almost everything in life is negotiable, from your cell phone bill to your salary. The only sure rule is that you're not going to get a better deal if you don't ask for it.

9. **Avoid Extra Fees:** These hide everywhere, including your bank account, your credit card, and your phone bill. Look for them everywhere, and cut them out everywhere you can.

10. **Reduce Your Tax Burden:** This is another topic that an entire book could be written on, but the truth is that a large part of your income vanishes every year. Speak to a professional or do some research on how you can reduce your tax burden in any way you can.

11. **Earn a Little Extra:** We all have the capacity to do this, but most of us don't. If you take a little extra and pour it into debt repayment or savings, it can make a drastic cumulative affect on your finances in a few years.

12. **Beware of Mutual Funds:** They're not all bad, but there are many of them out there that will destroy your profits with their fees. Keep an eye out for these, and stay away.

13. **Embrace Indexes:** These types of investments are a good way to build diversification into a portfolio when you don't have the capitol, or the experience to build it on your own by buying individual stocks.

14. **Pay Down the Highest Interest Debts First:** This one simple step alone can save you thousands of dollars in the long run.

15. **Be Wise With Budget Surpluses:** Don't use a surplus in your monthly budget as an excuse to go out for a night on the town. Pour that money into savings or debt repayment, and you can repair your financial well being even faster than you predicted.

16. **Repay Your Savings:** There will come a time when you have to utilize your savings for some kind of an emergency. That's what they're there for after all. Make sure to replenish the fund after you do, so that it is still there the next time you need it.

17. **Learn The Total Cost Of Ownership:** Learn this before you buy a car. There are many cars out there that look like a good deal because they're cheap, but poor reliability and the need for constant repairs can make them very

expensive after just a few years of ownership. A little research beforehand can save you thousands.

18. **Learn the Difference Between Good Debt and Bad:** This distinction can help you avoid some of the worst financial decisions that so many of us have made. There are times when it is okay to go into a little bit of debt, and times when it is not. Learning the difference is vital.

19. **Look after Your Health:** Doing so can directly save you money, and will make you much more capable of earning a good income and looking after your finances. The health of your body and your bank account are linked.

20. **Plan for the Worst, but Enjoy the Best:** If you plan for the worst case scenario, you will find yourself having frequent budget surpluses. That is a great place to find some money to roll into your savings fund that is going towards something fun for the whole family.

BONUS TIP

AVOID PAYDAY LENDERS: This is the last bonus piece of advice, because it is the most important. These companies use every ounce of marketing know-how they have to try and convince you that they're the best option when you're in a financial bind.

This couldn't be further from the truth, and I hope you'll use every resource at your disposal to try and stay away from these types of businesses. They're out to take advantage of people in a bad situation, and I hope that each and every one of you doesn't have to go through that.

Thanks again for reading, and good luck on your financial journey!

WAIT! – DO YOU LIKE FREE BOOKS?

My **FREE Gift** to You!! As a way to say **Thank You** for downloading my book, I'd like to offer you more **FREE BOOKS!** Each time we release a NEW book, we offer it first to a small number of people as a test–drive. Because of your commitment here in downloading my book, I'd love for you to be a part of this group. You can join easily here → **http://yourcashmanagement.com/**

Conclusion

Thank you again for downloading this book!

If you enjoyed this book, then I'd like to ask you for a favor, would you be kind enough to leave a review for this book on Amazon? It'd be greatly appreciated!

Help us better serve you by sending questions or comments to *greatreadspublishing@gmail.com*–Thank you!